AF227826

For Nate,

I pray you will know God's love for you .
I pray I can continue to teach you God's Word in a
way you can understand.

Love Mum x

Different and Wonderfully Made

Written and Illustrated
by Lisa McArthur-Collins

Copyright © 2026 Lisa McArthur-Collins

First Printing, 2026

Published by Little Wings Publishing
www.littlewingspublishing.com

ABN 29731392198

ISBN
978-1-7638789-4-5 Paperback
978-1-7638789-5-2 Hardcover

Different and Wonderfully Made

A 50-Day Devotional for Children Who Experience the World Differently

A Note for Parents and Caregivers:

This devotional was written for you to read with your child.
There is no right way to use this book.
You don't need to rush, explain, or finish every page.
Some days your child may sit and listen.
Some days they may move, stim, or wander away and that's okay.

Each day follows the same pattern:

Scripture - Adapted version, simpler to follow.
Devotional - For you to read to the child.
God's Truth - A short statement for the child.
Prayer - Perfect to close your devotional time.

Repetition is important for children. This is why we repeat the same pattern on every page.
Some of the devotional topics may also repeat themselves to help our children
learn through repetition.

You can read one line or the whole page.
You can pause, cuddle, or sit quietly together. Or read it on the trampoline!
God understands every sound, movement, and quiet or loud moment.
Above all, this book is here to remind you and your child of one simple truth:
God loves your child exactly as they are.

Lisa x

Wonder the Butterfly is hiding on every
page. Can you find her?
She reminds us that we are part of God's
beautiful creation.

Contents

Find What You Need For Today

When I Have Big Feelings

Day 9
Day 19
Day 30
Day 37
Day 41

When I Need Comfort

Day 11
Day 14
Day 42
Day 23
Day 27
Day 46

When I Feel Lonely

Day 5
Day 7
Day 11
Day 39
Day 44
Day 45
Day 50

When I Need A Reminder That I am Loved

Day 1
Day 3
Day 6
Day 7
Day 18
Day 27
Day 38
Day 43
Day 49

When I Feel Different

Day 4
Day 10
Day 13
Day 16
Day 44

When Communication Feels Hard

Day 6
Day 12
Day 28
Day 22
Day 36

When My Body Needs Extra Help

Day 15
Day 21
Day 26
Day 41

When I Make A Mistake

Day 31
Day 35

God Made You

God made you. Psalm 100:3

God made you.
He made your body and your mind.
He made you just the way
you are.
God doesn't make mistakes.
When God made you,
He smiled.

God
made
me on
purpose!

"Dear God,
Thank You
for making
me.
Amen."

2 ❤ God Loves You

God loves you very much. Romans 5:8

God loves you on happy days.
God loves you on hard days.
God loves you when you are loud.
God loves you when you are
quiet. God's love never
goes away.

"Dear God,
Thank You
for loving
me.
Amen."

God
loves
me
always!

 You Are Special

God made you special. Psalm 139:14

There is no one else like you.
God made you one of a kind.
You matter to God.
You are important.
God is happy you are here.

I am
special
to God!

"Dear God,
Thank You
for making
me special.
Amen."

4 Being Different Is Okay

God made each of us. Psalm 139:14

You might learn differently.
You might move differently.
And that's okay.
God made you.

Different is not wrong.

I'm different, and that's okay!

"Dear God,
Thank You
for how you
made me.
Amen."

God Is With You

God is with you. Joshua 1:9

God is with you in the morning.
God is with you at night.
God is with you everywhere you go.
You are never alone.
God stays close.

God
is
always
with
me!

6 God Knows You

God knows you. Psalm 139:1

God knows your name.
God knows your heart.
God knows what you need.
You don't have to explain
yourself to God.
God understands you.

God knows me!

"Dear God,
Thank You
for knowing
me.
Amen."

You Belong

You belong to God. 1 John 3:1

You belong in your family.
You belong with people who
care for you.
You belong to God.
There is a place for you.
You are wanted.

I belong
with
God!

"Dear God,
Thank You
that I
belong.
Amen."

 God Is Kind

God is kind. Psalm 145:9

God is gentle.
God is kind.
God is patient with you.
God is never mean.
God treats you with love.

God is kind to me!

"Dear God,
Thank You
for being
kind.
Amen."

9 God Understands Feelings

God understands us. Psalm 103:13

Sometimes feelings are big.
Sometimes feelings are hard.
God understands your feelings.
You can bring all your feelings to God.
God listens.

God understands
my feelings!

God Is Gentle

The Lord is gentle. Psalm 18:35

God speaks softly.
God moves slowly.
God is gentle with your heart.
You are safe with God.
God cares for you.

"Dear God, Thank You for being gentle. Amen."

 # 11 You Are Safe

God watches over you.
God cares for you.
God keeps you safe.
You can rest in God's care.
God is strong.

I am
safe with
God!

"Dear God,
Thank You
for keeping
me safe.
Amen."

♥ 12 God Hears You

God hears you. Psalm 34:17

God hears your words.
God hears your sounds.
God hears your heart.
Even when words are hard,
God listens.
God pays attention to you.

God
hears
me!

"Dear God,
Thank You
for hearing
me.
Amen."

13 God Is Patient

God is patient. 2 Peter 3:9

God is never in a rush.
God gives you time.
God waits with love.
You do not need to hurry.
God is patient
with you.

God is
patient
with
me!

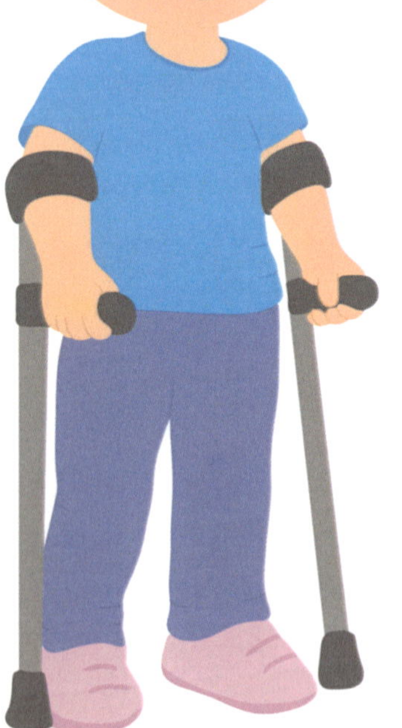

"Dear God,
Thank You
for being
patient.
Amen."

You Can Rest

Rest with God. Matthew 11:28

God invites you to rest.
You can slow down.
You can be still.
God is near when you rest.
You are allowed to rest.

I can rest with God!

"Dear God, Thank You for rest. Amen."

15 God Loves Your Body

Your body is God's. 1 Corinthians 6:19

God made your body.
God knows how your body works.
God loves your body just as it is.
Your body is good.
You are cared for.

God loves my body!

"Dear God, Thank You for my body. Amen."

God Loves How You Learn

God teaches us. Psalm 32:8

You may learn in your own way.
And that's okay.
God helps you learn.
God is proud of your efforts.
Trying is enough.

God helps me learn!

"Dear God,
Thank You
for helping
me learn.
Amen."

God Is Near

God is close. Psalm 34:18

God is close when you are happy.
God is close when you are sad.
God stays near.
You don't have to look far.
God is right here.

God is
close to
me!

"Dear God,
Thank You
for being
close.
Amen."

18 You Matter

You matter to God. Luke 12:7

You matter to your family.
You matter to others.
You matter to God.
Your life is important.
You are valued.

I matter!

 19 God Is Calm

God brings peace. John 14:27

God brings peace to busy minds.
God brings calm to big feelings.
God helps you slow down.
You can breathe with God.
God's peace is gentle.

God brings calm!

"Dear God, Thank You for Your peace. Amen."

20 God Delights In You

God delights in you. Psalm 149:4

God enjoys being with you.
God smiles over you.
You make God happy.
You do not need to earn God's love.
God delights in you.

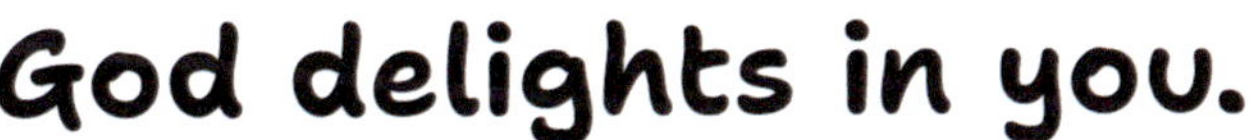

"Dear God,
Thank You for
delighting in
me.
Amen."

God Helps You

God helps you. Psalm 46:1

God helps you when things feel hard.
God helps you when you need support.
God sends people to help too.
You don't have to do
everything alone.
Help is okay.

God
helps
me!

"Dear God,
Thank You for
helping me.
Amen."

God Loves Your Voice

God listens. Psalm 66:19

Your voice matters.
Your sounds matter.
Your quiet matters.
God listens in every way.
You are heard.

God listens to me!

"Dear God, Thank You for listening. Amen."

 23 God Is Strong

God is strong. Psalm 28:7

God is stronger than fear.
God is stronger than worry.
God takes care of you.
You can trust God's strength.
God holds you.

God is strong for me!

"Dear God, Thank You for being strong. Amen."

God Is Trustworthy

God can be trusted. Proverbs 3:5

God keeps His promises.
God tells the truth.
God will not leave you.
You can trust God's love.
God is steady.

I can trust God!

"Dear God, Thank You that I can trust You. Amen."

 25 God Loves You Every Day

God's love lasts forever. Psalm 136:1

God loves you today.
God will love you tomorrow.
God's love does not stop.
Nothing can take God's love away.
You are always loved.

God loves me every day!

26 God Is Patient

God is slow to anger. Psalm 145:8

Some days are harder than others.
God does not rush you.
God stays calm with you.
You are safe with God.

"Dear God,
Thank You
for Your
patience.
Amen."

God Sees You

God sees you. Genesis 16:13

God sees you when others might not.
God notices you.
God pays attention to you.
You are not invisible.
You are seen and known.

God sees me!

"Dear God,
Thank You
for seeing
me.
Amen."

God Loves Quiet Moments

Be still. Psalm 46:10

God is with you in quiet moments.
You don't have to talk.
You don't have to move.
God enjoys being with you.
Quiet is okay.

**God is with me
in the quiet!**

"Dear God,
Thank You
for quiet
time.
Amen."

29 God Loves Joy

God gives joy. Psalm 16:11

God likes your smiles.
God likes your laughter.
God enjoys your joy.
Happy moments
matter to God.
Joy is a gift.

**God gives
me joy!**

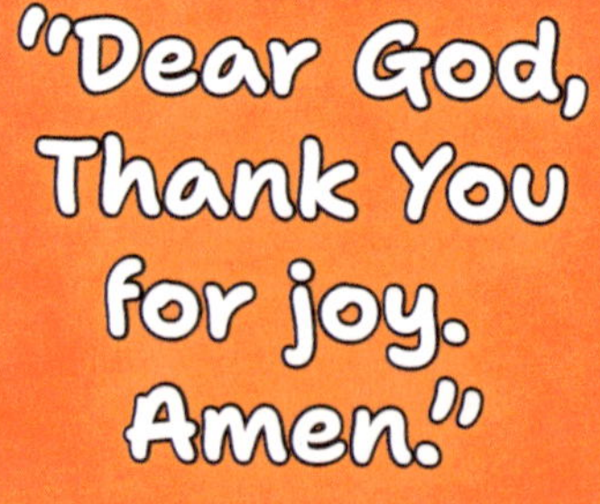

God Is With You When You Are Sad

God comforts you. 2 Corinthians 1:3

Sometimes you feel sad.

God stays with you.

God brings comfort.

You don't have to hide your sadness.

God cares for your heart.

God comforts me!

"Dear God, Thank You for comforting me. Amen."

God Loves Your Effort

God sees your work. Hebrews 6:10

You don't have to be perfect.
God sees when you try.
Trying matters to God.
God is proud of your effort.
You are doing enough.

Trying my best is enough!

"Dear God, Thank You for being proud of me. Amen."

God Loves Your Pace

The Lord guides you. Psalm 48:14

You can move slowly.
You can take breaks.
God walks with you.
Your pace is okay.
God is not in a hurry.

I can go
at my
pace!

"Dear God,
Thank You
for walking
with me.
Amen."

God Is Always Good

God is good. Psalm 34:8

God's heart is good.
God's plans are good.
God's love is good.
You can trust God's goodness.
God cares for you.

God is good to me!

God Loves Your Curiosity

Ask God. James 1:5

You can ask questions.
You can wonder.
God likes curious minds.
Questions are welcome with God.
God listens with love.

God welcomes
my questions!

"Dear God,
Thank You for
listening to my
questions.
Amen."

35 God Is Gentle With Mistakes

God forgives. 1 John 1:9

Everyone makes mistakes.
God is gentle when you do.
God helps you learn.
You are still loved.

Mistakes don't change
God's love for you.

Mistakes
are
okay!

"Dear God, Thank You for forgiving me. Amen."

God Loves How You Communicate

God knows your heart. Psalm 44:21

You may use words.
You may use actions.
You may use sounds.
God understands every way you communicate. You are understood.

God understands me!

"Dear God, Thank You for understanding me. Amen."

37 God Helps With Big Feelings

God helps you. Isaiah 41:10

Sometimes things feel too much.
God stays with you.
God helps you breathe.
You can take one moment at a time.
God is here.

God helps when things feel big!

"Dear God, Thank You for helping me. Amen."

38 God Loves You Just As You Are

God loves you. Jeremiah 31:3

You do not need to change for God.
You don't need to hide.
God loves you right now.
You are enough.
You are deeply loved.

God loves
me as
I am!

39 God Is Always Near

The Lord is near. Philippians 4:5

God is near in every place.
God is near in every feeling.
God doesn't leave.
You are held by God's presence.
You are not alone.

God is near!

"Dear God, Thank You for staying near. Amen."

40 God Loves You Deeply

Nothing can separate you.
Romans 8:38–39

Nothing can stop God's love.
Nothing can take it away.
God's love is strong.
God's love stays.
You are forever loved.

God's love never leaves!

"Dear God, Thank You for Your love. Amen."

41 God Cares About Your Needs

God cares about your body.
God cares about your feelings.
God cares about your needs.
You matter to God.
God helps provide what you need.

God cares for me!

God Is Calm And Steady

God is my peace. Psalm 29:11

God brings calm to busy days.
God brings peace to tired hearts.
You can slow down with God.
God is steady and kind.
You are safe.

**God helps me
feel calm!**

God Is Proud Of You

God delights in you. Zephaniah 3:17

God sees your efforts.
God sees your courage.
God sees you trying.
God is proud of you.
You are valued.

God is proud of me!

44 God Walks With You

God guides you. Psalm 73:24

God walks beside you.
God goes at your pace.
God does not push you.
You are not walking alone.
God is with you.

God walks with me!

"Dear God,
Thank You
for walking
with me.
Amen."

 45 God Is Always Loving

God is love. 1 John 4:8

God's heart is full of love.
God's words are loving.
God's actions are loving.
Love is who God is.
You are surrounded
by love.

God is love!

46 God Gives Comfort

God comforts you. Psalm 94:19

God gives comfort when you are tired.
God gives comfort when you are sad.
God holds you close.
You can rest in God's care.
Comfort is here.

God comforts me!

"Dear God, Thank You for Your comfort. Amen."

God Stays The Same

God does not change. Malachi 3:6

Some things change.
Some days feel different.
God stays the same.
God's love doesn't wobble
or move away.
You can rest knowing
God is the same.

God's love
does not
change!

"Dear God,
Thank You
for staying
the same.
Amen."

48 God Is Always Faithful

God is faithful. Lamentations 3:23

God keeps showing up.
God stays with you.
God doesn't forget you.
God is faithful.
You can trust God.

God will not leave me!

"Dear God, Thank You for staying with me. Amen."

You Are Deeply Loved

You are loved. Romans 8:39

You are loved on good days.
You are loved on hard days.
You are loved just as you are.
God's love surrounds you.
You are treasured.

I am deeply loved!

God Is With You Always

I am with you always. Matthew 28:20

God was with you yesterday.
God is with you today.
God will be with you tomorrow.
You are never alone.
God's love goes with you.

God is always with me!

"Dear God, Thank You for always being with me. Amen."

9 781763 878945